Lectin Free Cookbook Instant Pot

Lose Weight with Perfect Lectin-Free Recipes for Your Electric Pressure Cooker

Two Weeks Meal Planning for Fast Weight Loss

Tiffany Shelton

Disclaimer

The recipes and information in this book are provided for educational purposes only. Please always consult a licensed professional before making changes to your lifestyle or diet. The author and/or publisher shall have neither liability nor responsibility to anyone with respect to any loss or damage caused or alleged to be caused directly or indirectly by the information contained in this book. All trademarks and brands within this book are for clarifying purposes only and are owned by the owners themselves, not affiliated with this document.

Images from shutterstock.com

CONTENTS

INTRODUCTION

The world of dieting is a confusing one. Now we are now faced with such dieting issues as lectins. Before the discovery of lectins, we used to think all vegetables and fruits invariably were good for us and could be eaten in high amounts! But then lectins came under the spotlight, and everything changed! People soon started to realize that not all vegetables and fruits were safe to eat in the long run. Studies showed various links between longterm exposure to lectins and a wide array of different diseases such as diabetes, Alzheimer's, cancer, and sclerosis.

You might think that lectins are abundant in meats and processed foods, but you will be more surprised that it is abundant in raw grains and legumes. They are densely found in parts of the seed that become leaves when the plant germinates and turn to a sprout.

The invention of the Instant Pot has simplified cooking as it comes with tons of benefits. In this book, we will provide you with delicious Lectin-Free Instant Pot recipes so you will have a chance to prepare a wide range of lectin-free foods without subjecting yourself to stress.

CHAPTER 1. Instant Pot Basics

If you've never used Instant Pot before, here's what you need to know to get started right away.

Make sure the stainless-steel insert is clean and properly placed.

Wipe the outside of the stainless-steel pot with a dry towel to make sure nothing has stuck to the bottom or sides after you have placed it on the counter or in the sink. Stuck-on food or debris can interfere with the functioning of your pot, so make sure it's clean each time you use it.

Check that the silicone sealing ring is properly seated in the lid.

The silicone sealing ring expands from the heat and may move around when you take off the lid. Before securing the lid, use your fingers to gently wiggle the sealing ring all around the metal lid to ensure it is properly placed.

Make sure nothing is clogging the vent in your lid.

The stainless-steel cover over the vent is removable, so it's a good idea to clean it every now and then, especially after cooking pasta, to ensure no food or residue is blocking the vent.

Don't overfill the pot.

When cooking foods that are prone to foamings, such as beans or pasta, never fill the pot more than half full and always allow the pressure to naturally release as directed, so the foam doesn't spew out of the release vent. For other recipes, don't fill the pot more than two-thirds full.

Don't preheat the pot.

Although some people preheat the Instant Pot or start with very hot water to reduce the overall cooking time, the recipes in this book assume you are using cool water straight from your faucet or refrigerator. Cooking for less time than the recipes call for may result in your food not cooking as intended.

Don't place your pot directly underneath your kitchen cabinets.

In many cases, you'll need to manually release the steam pressure, which will shoot steam from the top of the pot. Be sure your Instant Pot is situated on a counter with nothing above it, so the hot steam doesn't do any damage.

Unplug your machine when you're done using it.

The Instant Pot goes into an automatic Keep Warm mode when the cooking cycle is complete, which is handy if you're not ready to serve yet. Be sure to unplug the device when you're done using it as a safety precaution.

Now that we've got that covered, here's how to:

Sauté.

The Instant Pot is unique in its ability to also sauté food. This means you can brown meat or sauté vegetables in the pot and then pressure cook in the same pot, or simmer excess liquid out of your sauce when the cooking cycle is over. To use the sauté function, simply press the Sauté button and wait for the beep that tells you the machine is on. Wait for 1 to 2 minutes after the beep for the surface to heat up before you add ingredients to the pot, or they may stick to the bottom. Do not use the lid when using this function; the lid should only be used when pressure cooking.

Cook on Manual.

Press the Manual or Pressure button, depending on your machine, then use the – or + buttons to set the appropriate cooking time. The Manual mode automatically cooks using high pressure, unless you press the Pressure button to switch to low pressure. When pressure cooking, always make sure the steam release valve is moved to the Sealing position. If your machine doesn't have a Manual setting, it most likely cooks on high pressure automatically.

Make sure the pressure has been reached.

There is a floating valve located on the lid next to the steam release valve that pops up when the pot has come to pressure. It usually takes anywhere from 5 to 20 minutes for the valve to pop up, depending on the recipe, and that's when the cooking cycle will begin counting down. Keep an eye on your Instant Pot until the floating valve has popped up to make sure your meal is cooking properly before walking away. You'll hear steam coming out of the vent shortly before the floating valve pops up.

Quickly release the pressure.

To avoid overcooking, many recipes require that you quickly release the pressure as soon as the Instant Pot has beeped to signal the end of a cooking cycle. To do that, carefully move the steam release valve to Venting, keeping your hand away from the top of the vent, so you don't get burned by the steam. As soon as the floating valve drops, remove the lid to stop the cooking process.

Naturally release the pressure.

Allow the lid to remain on the Instant Pot after the cooking cycle has ended until the specified time has passed. Once the cooking cycle has counted down, the timer will start again, counting *up* the minutes to let you know how long it's been since the cooking cycle stopped. If a recipe requires that you let the pressure naturally release for 10 minutes, don't touch the lid until your Instant Pot reads Lo:10, which means it has been on a "keep warm" setting for 10 minutes. When the time has passed, move the steam release valve to the Venting position to release any remaining steam before you remove the lid.

Know that it's safe to remove the lid.

After using a quick or natural release and venting any remaining steam in the pot, the floating valve on the lid, which is next to the steam release valve, will drop, letting you know that all of the pressure has been released. The lid has a safety feature that won't let you open it until the valve has dropped.

Use the pot-in-pot cooking method.

This refers to cooking two dishes at the same time, using a separate bowl that fits inside the Instant Pot. To use this time-saving method, you'll need a 2.5-inch trivet and a 7-inch oven-safe bowl that is placed on the trivet over the main entrée, which is cooked directly on the bottom of the Instant Pot. Both the main entrée and the side dish need to cook a similar amount of time for best results.

Cook for 0 (zero) minutes.

Though it might sound strange, some recipes require that you set the pressure cooking cycle for 0 (zero) minutes to ensure that you don't overcook your ingredients. This cooking cycle simply brings the pot to pressure, which can take anywhere from 5 to 20 minutes, and when it beeps and displays Lo:00 on the screen, you quickly release the pressure by moving the steam release valve to Venting. Releasing the pressure can take 1 to 2 minutes more, so the food will be sufficiently cooked despite the short cooking time.

If you run into problems, the following tips should help:

✓ **I've selected the cooking program, but my pot just says "on." Why hasn't the countdown started yet?**

After you select your cooking program and cooking time, the Instant Pot waits 10 seconds to start. When it beeps, you'll see an "On" message as it starts to come to pressure. The cooking cycle won't start counting down until the pot is pressurized, and that process can take anywhere from 5 to 20 minutes after you set the timer, depending on how much liquid is in the pot. The less liquid, the faster it will come to pressure.

✓ **How do I adjust the cooking time and pressure setting?**

After selecting the Manual or Pressure button, use the − and + buttons to adjust the time. The Manual setting cooks at high pressure automatically, but you can press the Pressure button to adjust the pressure to low on certain models.

✓ **Will these recipes work for an 8-quart Instant Pot?**

All of these recipes have been successfully tested using the 8-quart Instant Pot Duo. When using this size pot, follow the recipe directions closely, as the 8-quart is prone to displaying "Burn" errors. In any recipe that calls for sautéing meat or vegetables first, always deglaze the pan before bringing the pot to pressure, so nothing sticks to the bottom. You can do this by adding a splash of water to the hot pan, then using a wooden spoon or spatula to scrape the bottom of the pan to remove anything that has stuck. Recipes don't always need a full cup of added liquid to make this model come to pressure, but you do need to make sure the ingredients are layered in the correct order to avoid burn errors. Also, keep in mind that vegetables might lose their crunch when cooked in this pot due to the longer pressurization time.

✓ **Do I need to adjust the cooking time if I double the recipe?**

In most cases, you can double a recipe without changing the cooking time, but keep in mind that the increased volume will naturally increase the overall time it takes to prepare the dish because the Instant Pot may take longer to come to pressure. If you're using particularly large cuts of meat, such as large or frozen chicken breasts, they may need a few minutes more to cook. Don't fill your pot more than half full for items that produce foam (like pasta or beans) and more than two-thirds full for everything else.

✓ My Instant Pot never came to pressure. What happened?

If your Instant Pot has been on for more than 25 minutes and the floating valve hasn't popped up to signal that the pressure has been reached, check to make sure you've moved the steam release to Sealing. If that's not the issue, it could be that the sealing ring in the lid has moved and isn't sealing, or that something was stuck to the bottom of your pot, triggering the "Burn" error.

✓ I see a "Burn" error on my Instant Pot. What should I do?

The "Burn" or "Hot" message on the Instant Pot means that the bottom surface of the stainless-steel pot is getting too hot. This can happen when your Instant Pot is empty, when you're heating the pot to sauté something, and when food gets stuck to the bottom of the pot during the cooking process. To remove stuck food, add a splash of water to the hot pan and use a wooden spoon to scrape the bottom until nothing is stuck. The error message will go away quickly, and you can continue with your recipe as directed. Also, be sure that you have moved the steam release valve to Sealing, so the liquid in your pot doesn't evaporate as it heats up during a pressure cooking cycle.

✓ The floating valve dropped in the middle of a cooking cycle. What should I do?

If steam is coming out of your Instant Pot's floating valve *after* the pressure cooking cycle has started counting down, that means the pot is no longer pressurized, and your meal isn't cooking properly. If you can, gently grab the lid by its handle (don't touch the metal as it's very hot) and press down to see if the lid will seal and pop the valve back up. Sometimes, that's all it takes. If the valve doesn't pop up, you'll need to press Cancel, move the steam release valve to Venting to make sure the pressure is fully released, and remove the lid. Add a bit more liquid to the pot, starting with just ¼ cup water if it looks like there is plenty of liquid at the bottom, or using more if it looks like much of the cooking liquid has simmered away. Use a wooden spoon to scrape the bottom of the pot, making sure nothing has stuck, then close the lid, move the steam release valve to Sealing, and start the pressure cooking process again. Use your best judgment on the timing based on how much cooking time was left in the cycle when the pressure was lost.

✓ Steam is coming out around the rim of my lid. What should I do?

If you see steam coming out around the rim of your lid, and not just from the steam release valve, that is a sign that something is wrong with your sealing ring. You'll have to press Cancel, move the steam release valve to Venting to make sure the pressure is fully released, and remove the lid to check the sealing ring. It's not uncommon for the sealing ring to expand from the heat and move out of place, breaking the seal, so you may be able to fix this issue by pushing the ring back into place and sealing the lid again to continue pressure cooking. If the sealing ring appears to be cracked or damaged, you'll need to buy a replacement.

✓ Why won't my Instant Pot open?

The Instant Pot is designed to stay closed as a safety precaution when the pot is coming to pressure, so you can't open it until the floating valve has dropped. Before attempting to remove the lid, remember to move the steam release valve to Venting and wait for all of the steam to release and the floating valve to drop.

Now that we've covered the basics let's get cooking!

CHAPTER 2. 14-Day Meal Plan

Week 1

	Breakfast	Lunch	Snack	Dinner
Day 1	Authentic Baked Apple Page 18	Beet and Carrot Soup Page 32	Garlic Rose Page 23	Sweet Chili Tilapia Platter Page 38
Day 2	Hard Boiled Eggs Page 14	Mixed Veggie with Portobello Mushrooms Soup Page 29	Amazing Pickle Jar Page 22	Italian Chicken Dish Page 45
Day 3	Amazing Prosciutto Cane Page 13	Carrot Soup Page 30	Garlic and Broccoli Platter Page 24	Harissa Beef Page 52
Day 4	The Up-Beat Instant Broccoli Page 16	Celery Soup Page 34	Warm Curried Mushrooms Page 25	Majestic Pepper Steak Page 55
Day 5	Mexican Guacamole Page 19	Beet Borscht Page 37	Feisty Carrot and Kale Platter Page 27	Artichoke and Lemon Pork Chops Page 58
Day 6	Unique Sweet Potatoes Delight Page 15	Apple and Broccoli Soup Page 36	Zucchini and Artichoke Dish Page 26	Caramelized Onion Chicken Page 47
Day 7	Cauliflower Mash Page 17	Cauliflower and Sage Soup Page 35	Garlic and Broccoli Platter Page 24	Lemon Pepper Chicken and Cauliflower Scrambl Page 50

	Breakfast	Lunch	Snack	Dinner
Day 8	Authentic Baked Apple Page 18	Beet and Carrot Soup Page 32	Amazing Pickle Jar Page 22	Capsicum Braised Pork Page 56
Day 9	Mexican Guacamole Page 19	Apple and Broccoli Soup Page 36	Garlic and Broccoli Platter Page 24	Feisty Poached Salmon Page 40
Day 10	Hard Boiled Eggs Page 14	Carrot Soup Page 30	Warm Curried Mushrooms Page 25	Kale Salad and Salmon Page 43
Day 11	Amazing Prosciutto Cane Page 13	Celery Soup Page 34	Feisty Carrot and Kale Platter Page 27	Salsa Chicken Breast Page 46
Day 12	Unique Sweet Potatoes Delight Page 15	Beet Borscht Page 37	Zucchini and Artichoke Dish Page 26	Orange Chicken Page 49
Day 13	Cauliflower Mash Page 17	Cauliflower and Sage Soup Page 35	Garlic Rose Page 23	Red Wine Braised Beef Shorts Page 57
Day 14	The Up-Beat Instant Broccoli Page 16	Mixed Veggie with Portobello Mushrooms Soup Page 29	Garlic and Broccoli Platter Page 24	Pineapple Pork Chops Page 59

CHAPTER 3. Recipes

BREAKFAST

Amazing Prosciutto Cane

Prep time: 10 minutes

Cooking time: 20 minutes

Servings: 4

Nutrients per serving:

Carbohydrates – 11 g

Fat – 14 g

Protein – 12 g

Calories – 212

Ingredients:

- 1 pound thick asparagus
- 5 lb.prosciutto, sliced

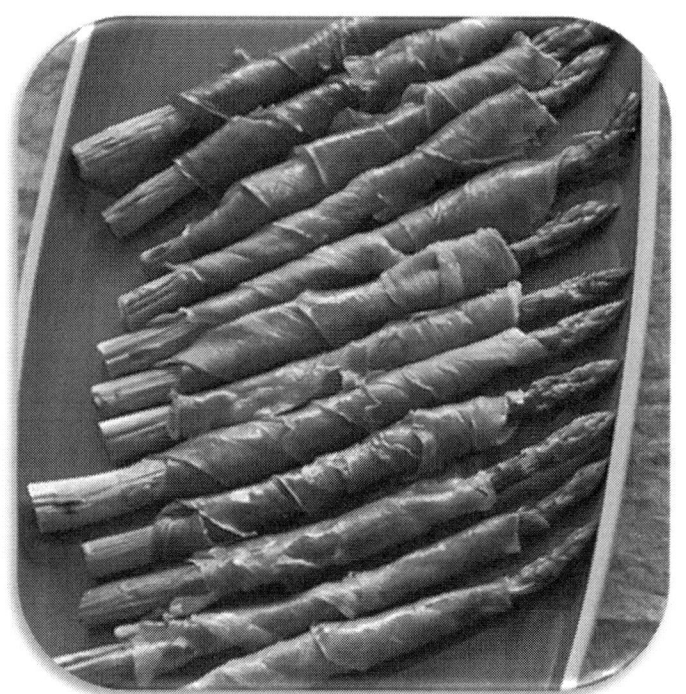

Instructions:

1. Wrap and roll the asparagus spear in a spiral like a candy cane stripe up to the top of the spear. Continue with the others. Add it to your Instant Pot.
2. Lock the lid. Cook on HIGH pressure for 20 minutes.
3. Release pressure naturally over 10 minutes Serve.

Hard Boiled Eggs

Prep time: 1 minute

Cooking time: 5 minutes

Servings: 4

Nutrients per serving:

Carbohydrates – 1 g

Fat – 5 g

Protein – 7 g

Calories – 81

Ingredients:

- 4 eggs
- 1 cup water

Instructions:

1. Place a trivet in your Instant Pot.
2. Arrange eggs in a layer and add a cup of water. Lock the lid. Cook on HIGH pressure for 5 minutes.
3. Quick release pressure. Transfer eggs to cold water and peel. Serve.

Unique Sweet Potatoes Delight

Prep time: 15 minutes

Cooking time: 10 minutes

Servings: 4

Nutrients per serving:

Carbohydrates – 30 g

Fat – 19 g

Protein – 33 g

Calories – 442

Ingredients:

- 2 cups water
- 4 sweet potatoes, peeled, sliced
- 2 Tbsp coconut oil
- 1 whole onion, julienned
- ¼ cup vegetable broth
- 2 Tbsp fresh lemon juice
- ¼ cup of parsley
- Salt, pepper, to taste

Instructions:

1. Add water and potatoes to Instant Pot.
2. Lock the lid. Cook on HIGH pressure for 5 minutes.
3. Release pressure naturally over 10 minutes.
4. Drain potatoes into a colander.
5. Add coconut oil to the pot and set the pot to Saute mode. Let it heat up.
6. Add potatoes, lemon juice, and broth.
7. Saute for 5 minutes.
8. Remove heat.
9. Stir in parsley and season with salt and pepper. Serve.

The Up-Beat Instant Broccoli

Prep time: 15 minutes

Cooking time: 2 minutes

Servings: 2

Nutrients per serving:

Carbohydrates – 2 g

Fat – 3 g

Protein – 1 g

Calories – 33

Ingredients:

- ¾ cup water
- 1 medium broccoli
- Salt, pepper, to taste

Instructions:

1. Add water to Instant Pot.
2. Chop broccoli into florets and transfer to a steamer rack.
3. Place steamer rack on top of your Instant Pot. Lock the lid. Cook on HIGH pressure for 2 minutes.
4. Release pressure naturally over 10 minutes. Season with salt and pepper and serve.

Cauliflower Mash

Prep time: 15 minutes

Cooking time: 5 minutes

Servings: 4

Nutrients per serving:

Carbohydrates – 4 g

Fat – 0.6 g

Protein – 8 g

Calories – 249

Ingredients:

- 1½ cups of water
- 2 pound sweet potatoes, peeled, sliced in 1 inch pieces
- 8 ounce cauliflower florets
- ½ a tsp salt
- 1 garlic clove, minced

Instructions:

1. Add water to Instant Pot.
2. Add florets and potatoes and lock the lid.
3. Cook on HIGH pressure for 5 minutes.
4. Release the pressure naturally.
5. Season with salt and garlic.
6. Mash the whole mix. Serve.

Authentic Baked Apple

Prep time: 15 minutes

Cooking time: 10 minutes

Servings: 6

Nutrients per serving:

Carbohydrates – 45 g

Fat – 17 g

Protein – 3 g

Calories – 332

Ingredients:

- 6 fresh apples
- ¼ cup raisins
- 1 cup red wine vinegar
- 1 tsp cinnamon powder

Instructions:

1. Add all ingredients to Instant Pot.
2. Lock the lid and cook on HIGH pressure for 10 minutes.
3. Release the pressure naturally over 10 minutes.
4. Scoop out into bowls. Serve.

Mexican Guacamole

Prep time: 5 minutes

Cooking time: 5 minutes

Servings: 6

Nutrients per serving:

Carbohydrates – 3.1 g

Fat – 4.4 g

Protein – -0.7 g

Calories – 50

Ingredients:

- 1 large sized avocado
- ¼ finely chopped red onion
- ½ of a juiced lime
- 1 finely chopped sprig cilantro
- Salt, to taste

Instructions:

1. Halve up the avocado and gently remove the pit.
2. Run a knife vertically and horizontally through the flesh.
3. Take a spoon and scoop out the cubed avocado pieces form the skin and transfer to a bowl.
4. Take a fork and mash the avocado.
5. Add lime juice, cilantro and lime, and onion. Serve!

SNACKS

Fancy Assorted Brussels Collection

Prep time: 20 minutes

Cooking time: 3 minutes

Servings: 2

Nutrients per serving:

Carbohydrates – 22 g

Fat – 7 g

Protein – 6 g

Calories – 197

Ingredients:

- 1 pound Brussels sprouts
- ¼ cup pine nuts, toasted
- 1 Tbsp extra-virgin olive oil
- ½ tsp salt
- 1 pepper, grated

Instructions:

1. Remove the outer leaves of the Brussels sprouts and trim stems.
2. Wash Brussels sprouts thoroughly and cut the largest ones in half. Cut the others in uniform size.
3. Pour in a cup of water to the Instant Pot.
4. Place a steamer basket in the pot and add the sprouts.
5. Lock the lid. Cook on HIGH pressure for 3 minutes.
6. Release pressure naturally over 10 minutes and transfer sprouts to serving a dish.
7. Toss with olive oil, salt, pepper, and pine nuts. Serve

Subtle Braised Cabbage

Prep time: 15 minutes

Cooking time: 3 minutes

Servings: 6

Nutrients per serving:

Carbohydrates – 7 g

Fat – 10 g

Protein – 3 g

Calories – 70

Ingredients:

- 1 Tbsp clarified butter
- 1 head green cabbage, cored, quartered and cut into ½ inch strips
- 1 cup vegetable broth
- Salt, fresh ground black pepper, to taste

Instructions:

1. Set your pot to Saute mode.
2. Combine all ingredients in a pot.
3. Lock the lid. Cook on HIGH pressure for 3 minutes.
4. Quick release pressure. Serve.

Amazing Pickle Jar

Prep time: 15 minutes

Cooking time: 10 minutes

Servings: 4

Nutrients per serving:

Carbohydrates – 35 g

Fat – 14 g

Protein – 8 g

Calories – 293

Ingredients:

- 1 pound green chilies
- 1½ cups apple cider vinegar
- 1 tsp pickling salt
- 1½ tsp date paste
- ¼ tsp garlic powder

Instructions:

1. Add ingredients to Instant Pot
2. Lock the lid. Cook on HIGH pressure for about 10 minutes
3. Release pressure naturally over 10 minutes
4. Spoon mix into washed jars and cover slices with cooking liquid
5. Serve.

GarlicRose

Prep time: 15 minutes

Cooking time: 1 hour

Servings: 4

Nutrients per serving:

Carbohydrates – 19 g

Fat – 16 g

Protein – 9 g

Calories – 254

Ingredients:

- 3 whole large garlic bulbs
- 1 Tbsp extra virgin olive oil
- 1 cup water

Instructions:

1. Place a steamer rack in Pot.
2. Add water and slice garlic bulbs into ¼ portions.
3. Lock the lid. Cook on HIGH pressure for 6 minutes.
4. Release pressure naturally over 10 minutes.
5. Use tongs to take the bulbs out.
6. Transfer them to an oven safe dish.
7. Drizzle oil on top and broil in oven for 55 minutes. Serve.

Garlic and Broccoli Platter

Prep time: 15 minutes

Cooking time: 11 minutes

Servings: 4

Nutrients per serving:

Carbohydrates – 6 g

Fat – 8 g

Protein – 6 g

Calories – 101

Ingredients:

- 2 whole broccoli heads, cut into florets
- ½ cup water
- 6 cloves garlic, minced
- 1 Tbsp olive oil
- 1 Tbsp white wine vinegar
- Salt, to taste

Instructions:

1. Take a steamer rack and place it in Instant Pot.
2. Add florets to the rack.
3. Lock lid and cook on LOW for 10 minutes.
4. Transfer floret to the ice bath and let them cool.
5. Discard water from Instant Pot and set your pot to Saute mode.
6. Add 1 Tbsp olive oil and add minced garlic.
7. Saute for 1 minute and add broccoli.
8. Add 1 Tbsp white vinegar.
9. Season with salt and stir for 1 minute. Serve.

Warm Curried Mushrooms

Prep time: 15 minutes

Cooking time: 4 minutes

Servings: 2

Nutrients per serving:

Carbohydrates – 71 g

Fat – 7 g

Protein – 37 g

Calories – 486

Ingredients:

- 1 lb mushrooms of your choice
- 6 whole garlic cloves, peeled and crushed
- ¼ cup red wine vinegar
- ½ cup mushroom stock
- 2 tsp coconut aminos
- Black pepper, to taste
- 1 Tbsp browning sauce

Instructions:

1. Add ingredients to Instant Pot.
2. Lock the lid. Cook on HIGH pressure for 4 minutes.
3. Serve hot.

Zucchini and Artichoke Dish

Prep time: 15 minutes

Cooking time: 15 minutes

Servings: 2

Nutrients per serving:

Carbohydrates – 2 g

Fat – 3 g

Protein – 0.57 g

Calories – 33

Ingredients:

- 2 Tbsp coconut oil
- 1 bulb garlic, minced
- 1 large artichoke heart, cleaned sliced
- 2 medium zucchinis, sliced
- ½ cup vegetable broth
- Salt and pepper, to taste

Instructions:

1. Set pot to Saute mode and add oil. Let the oil heat up.
2. Add garlic and Saute until fragrant.
3. Add remaining ingredients and gently stir.
4. Lock the lid. Cook on HIGH pressure for about 10 minutes.
5. Quick release pressure and serve.

Feisty Carrot and Kale Platter

Prep time: 15 minutes

Cooking time: 15 minutes

Servings: 2

Nutrients per serving:

Carbohydrates – 2 g

Fat – 3 g

Protein – 0.57 g

Calories – 33

Ingredients:

- 10 ounces kale, chopped
- 1 Tbsp olive oil
- 1 medium onion, thinly sliced
- 3 medium carrots, cut into ½ inch slices
- 5 garlic cloves, peeled and roughly chopped
- ½ cup chicken broth
- Salt and pepper, to taste
- 2 tsp aAged balsamic vinegar
- ¼ tsp red pepper flakes

Instructions:

1. Set the pot to Saute mode and add olive oil.
2. Add carrots and onion and Saute for a few minutes.
3. Add garlic and stir for 30 seconds.
4. Add kale, vegetable broth, salt, and pepper.
5. Lock the lid and cook on HIGH pressure for 5 minutes.
6. Release the pressure naturally and stir.
7. Top with a bit of balsamic vinegar and red pepper flakes. Serve.

Sweet and Spicy Carrot

Prep time: 10 minutes

Cooking time: 5 minutes

Servings: 4

Nutrients per serving:

Carbohydrates – 20 g

Fat – 4 g

Protein – 1 g

Calories – 74

Ingredients:

- 1 cup water
- 5-6 large carrots, peeled and cut into 1-inch chunks
- 1 Tbsp clarified butter
- ¼ tsp ground cumin
- ¼ tsp cayenne
- Salt, pepper, to taste
- 2 tsp honey

Instructions:

1. Add water to Instant Pot.
2. Place a steamer basket on top. Then add carrots.
3. Lock lid and STEAM for 2 minutes on high pressure.
4. Quick release pressure.
5. Remove steamer basket and discard water.
6. Dry the pot and place it in the Instant Pot again.
7. Add clarified butter to Instant pot and set it to Saute mode.
8. Add carrots to the pot and stir until coated.
9. Add cumin, cayenne and season with salt and pepper. Stir well.
10. Add in honey and Cancel Saute. Serve.

SOUPS AND SALADS

Mixed Veggie with Portobello Mushrooms Soup

Prep time: 10 minutes

Cooking time: 15 minutes

Servings: 10

Nutrients per serving:

Carbohydrates – 18.6 g

Fat – 3.1 g

Protein – 4 g

Calories – 117

Ingredients:

- 2 Tbsp olive oil
- 1 carrot, peeled and minced
- 1 celery stalk, minced
- 1 small onion, minced
- 2 garlic cloves, minced
- 1 tsp dried rosemary, crushed
- 8 oz Portobello mushrooms, sliced
- 8 oz white mushrooms, sliced
- ½ cup red wine
- 2 Yukon Gold potatoes, peeled and chopped
- 1½ cups fresh green beans, trimmed and chopped roughly
- 1 Tbsp balsamic vinegar
- 3 cups water
- 2 Tbsp cornstarch
- Salt, pepper, to taste
- 4 ounce peas, frozen
- ¾ cup pearl onions

Instructions:

1. Pour the oil in the Instant Pot and select Sauté.
2. Add carrots, celery, and onion, and cook for about 2-3 minutes. Stir in garlic and rosemary and cook for 1 minute.
3. Next, add mushrooms and cook for about 4-5 minutes. Pour in the wine and cook for 2 minutes, scraping the brown bits from the bottom.
4. Select "Cancel" and stir in carrots, potatoes, green beans, vinegar, and water. Next, secure the lid and cook under "Manual" and "High Pressure" for about 15 minutes.
5. Select "Cancel" and carefully do a quick release.
6. In a bowl, dissolve cornstarch into water.
7. Remove Instant Pot lid and stir in cornstarch mixture, salt, black pepper, peas, and pearl onions. Select "Sauté" and cook for about 1 minute. Serve hot.

Carrot Soup

Prep time: 15 minutes

Cooking time: 20 minutes

Servings: 4

Nutrients per serving:

Carbohydrates – 35 g

Fat – 1 g

Protein – 3 g

Calories – 147

Ingredients:

- 1 Tbsp ghee
- ½ yellow onion, chopped
- 3 cloves garlic, minced
- 1 Tbsp curry powder
- 1 tsp cayenne pepper
- 1½ cups vegetable broth
- 8-10 large carrots, peeled and chopped
- 1 14-oz can unsweetened coconut milk

Instructions:

1. Set Instant Pot to Saute mode and add ghee, let it heat up.
2. Add onion and garlic and Saute for about 5 minutes.
3. Add remaining ingredients and stir.
4. Lock the lid. Cook on HIGH pressure for 15 minutes.
5. Release naturally over 10 minutes.
6. Open the lid and use an immersion blender to smoothen the soup. Serve.

Leek and Broccoli Soup

Prep time: 25 minutes

Cooking time: 12 minutes

Servings: 4

Nutrients per serving:

Carbohydrates – 29 g

Fat – 8 g

Protein – 7 g

Calories – 194

Ingredients:

- 2 Tbsp ghee
- 3 medium leeks, white parts only
- 2 shallots, chopped
- 1 large head broccoli, cut up into florets
- 4 cups vegetable broth
- 1 cup unsweetened coconut milk
- Pepper, salt, to taste
- ¼ cup toasted walnuts
- ¼ cup coconut cream

Instructions:

1. Set Instant Pot to Saute mode and add ghee, let it heat up.
2. Add leeks and shallots and cook for 4-6 minutes.
3. Add broccoli and Saute for 5-6 minutes.
4. Release pressure naturally over 10 minutes.
5. Open the lid and puree the soup using immersion blender.
6. Garnish with toasted walnuts and drizzle of coconut cream. Serve.

Beet and Carrot Soup

Prep time: 20 minutes

Cooking time: 20 minutes

Servings: 4

Nutrients per serving:

Carbohydrates – 20 g

Fat – 2 g

Protein – 2 g

Calories – 102

Ingredients:

- 1 Tbsp ghee
- ½ yellow onion, chopped
- 3 cloves garlic, minced
- 1 Tbsp curry powder
- 1 tsp cayenne pepper
- 1½ cups vegetable broth
- 8-10 large carrots, peeled and chopped
- 1 14-oz can unsweetened coconut milk

Instructions:

1. Set Instant Pot to Saute mode and add ghee, allow the ghee to heat up.
2. Add in onion and garlic and cook for about 5 minutes.
3. Add rest of the ingredients, except coconut milk, and stir.
4. Lock the lid and cook on HIGH pressure for 15 minutes.
5. Release the pressure naturally over 10 minutes.
6. Open and puree using immersion blender
7. Stir in unsweetened coconut milk. Serve.

Beet Salad

Prep time: 25 minutes

Cooking time: 1 minute

Servings: 6

Nutrients per serving:

Carbohydrates – 13 g

Fat – 7 g

Protein – 2 g

Calories – 120

Ingredients:

- 6 medium sized beets
- 1 cup water
- Kosher salt, black pepper, to taste
- ½ tsp balsamic vinegar
- 1 Tbsp extra virgin olive oil

Instructions:

1. Wash beets thoroughly and trim to ½ inch cubes.
2. Pour in a cup of water to the Instant Pot.
3. Place a steamer/trivet in the pot and arrange the beets on top.
4. Lock the lid. Cook on HIGH pressure for 1 minute.
5. Release pressure naturally over 10 minutes.
6. Let the beets cool.
7. Season with salt and pepper.
8. Add vinegar and let the beets marinate for 30 minutes.
9. Add a bit of extra olive oil and serve.

Celery Soup

Prep time: 25 minutes

Cooking time: 24 minutes

Servings: 3

Nutrients per serving:

Carbohydrates – 20 g

Fat – 13 g

Protein – 6 g

Calories – 214

Ingredients:

- 1 large celery root finely chopped into 4-5 cups
- 1 medium sized chopped onion
- 4 peeled garlic cloves
- 3 cups vegetable broth, divided
- 1/8 tsp white pepper
- ½ tsp thyme
- ½ tsp salt
- ¼ cup almond milk
- ½ tsp lemon juice

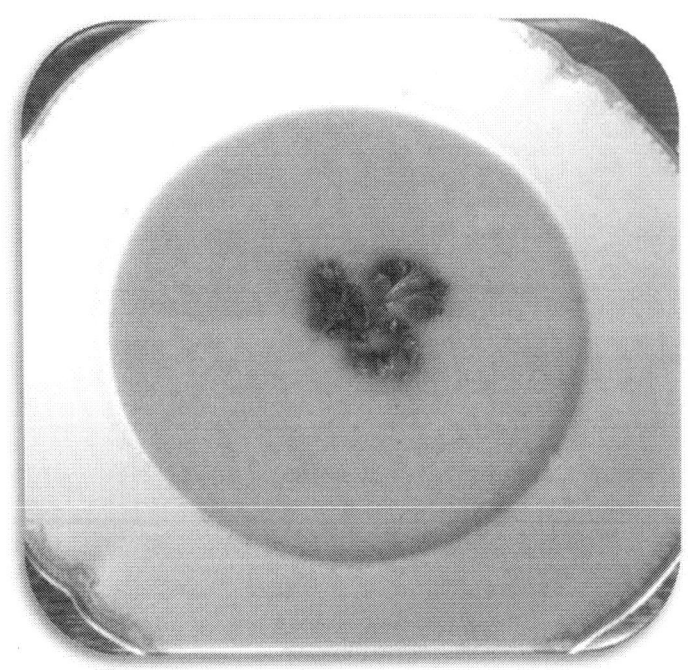

Instructions:

1. Peel celery root and cut into equal cubes.
2. Set pot to Saute mode and brown onion and garlic.
3. Add celery root and broth, and lock lid.
4. Cook on HIGH pressure for 4 minutes.
5. Release pressure naturally over 10 minutes.
6. Open the lid and blend with immersion blender until you have your desired consistency.
7. Add white pepper, thyme, and salt.
8. Set your pot to Saute mode and simmer for 20 minutes.
9. Add almond milk and lemon juice and stir for 5 minutes.
10. Serve.

Cauliflower and Sage Soup

Prep time: 20 minutes

Cooking time: 16 minutes

Servings: 4

Nutrients per serving:

Carbohydrates – 43 g

Fat – 18 g

Protein – 18 g

Calories – 412

Ingredients:

- 1 tsp olive oil
- 1 onion, chopped
- 4 cloves garlic, minced
- 1 Tbsp fresh sage
- 8 cups cauliflower florets
- 3 cups chicken broth
- ½ tsp salt
- Pepper, to taste
- ½ cup unsweetened coconut milk

Instructions:

1. Set Instant Pot to Saute mode and add olive oil, let it heat up.
2. Add onion and cook for 3-5 minutes.
3. Stir in garlic and sage, and cook for 1 minute.
4. Add cauliflower, broth, salt, and pepper. Stir well.
5. Lock the lid. Cook on HIGH pressure for 10 minutes.
6. Release pressure naturally over 10 minutes.
7. Puree using immersion blender.
8. Stir in unsweetened coconut milk. Serve.

Apple and Broccoli Soup

Prep time: 20 minutes

Cooking time: 15 minutes

Servings: 4

Nutrients per serving:

Carbohydrates – 5 g

Fat – 8 g

Protein – 0 g

Calories – 160

Ingredients:

- 2 Tbsp olive oil
- The white parts of 3 medium sized leeks
- 2 medium shallots, chopped
- 1 Tbsp Indian curry powder
- Kosher salt
- 1½ lb chopped broccoli
- ¼ cup green apple, peeled, diced
- 4 cups vegetable broth
- Freshly ground black pepper, to taste
- 1 cup full fat coconut milk

Instructions:

1. Set pot to Saute mode and add oil, allow to heat up.
2. Add vegetables and Saute them.
3. Add curry powder and salt.
4. Stir well, until aromatic.

5. Add apple and broccoli and stir well.
6. Cover veggies with vegetable broth.
7. Lock the lid and cook on HIGH pressure for 5 minutes.
8. Release the pressure naturally.
9. With an immersion blender, blend the mixture well until you have a soupy consistency.
10. Add coconut milk, a bit more salt, and pepper. Blend well and serve.

Beet Borscht

Prep time: 25 minutes

Cooking time: 55 minutes

Servings: 4

Nutrients per serving:

Carbohydrates – 43 g

Fat – 9 g

Protein – 8 g

Calories – 268

Ingredients:

- 3 large beets, peeled
- 3 stalks celery, diced
- 3 large carrots, diced
- 2 large garlic, diced
- 1 medium onion, diced
- 3 cups cabbage, shredded
- 6 cups vegetable stock
- 1 Tbsp salt
- Bay leaf
- ½ Tbsp thyme
- ¼ cup fresh dill, chopped
- 1 cup water

Instructions:

1. Add beets to a steamer and place steamer in Instant Pot.
2. Add a cup of water.
3. Lock lid and STEAM for 7 minutes
4. Quick release pressure.
5. Drop the beets into an ice bath.
6. Add cooled beets and remaining ingredients to the Instant Pot.
7. Lock lid and cook on SOUP mode for 45 minutes.
8. Naturally release pressure over 10 minutes.
9. Ladle into bowls and serve.

FISH AND SEAFOOD

Sweet Chili Tilapia Platter

Prep time: 25 minutes

Cooking time: 5 minutes

Servings: 4

Nutrients per serving:

Carbohydrates – 1 g

Fat – 4 g

Protein – 21 g

Calories – 118

Ingredients:

- 4 Tilapia fish fillets, boneless, skinless
- 2 tsp olive oil
- ¼ cup coconut aminos
- Salt and pepper, to taste
- 2 tsp crushed red pepper flakes
- 2 tsp low-sodium coconut aminos
- ¼ cup homemade Lectin-Free Chili Sauce
- 2 scallions, green parts only, finely sliced

Instructions:

1. In a bowl, combine 1 tsp coconut aminos, red pepper flakes, black pepper, and salt.
2. Mix well and coat the fillets with the marinade.
3. In a separate bowl, combine chili sauce and remaining aminos.
4. Set your pot to Saute mode and add olive oil, allow to heat up.
5. Add fillets and Saute for 2-3 minutes per side.
6. Transfer fillets to serving platter.
7. Top with chili sauce mix and serve.

Salmon and Broccoli Platter

Prep time: 25 minutes

Cooking time: 5 minutes

Servings: 4

Nutrients per serving:

Carbohydrates – 1 g

Fat – 4 g

Protein – 21 g

Calories – 701

Ingredients:

- 2½ oz salmon fillets
- 2½ oz broccoli, chopped in florets
- 1 tsp almond butter
- Pepper, to taste
- 1 tsp crushed sunflower seeds
- ½ cup water

Instructions:

1. Add ½ cup water to your Instant Pot.
2. Season salmon and broccoli florets with sunflower seeds and pepper.
3. Add broccoli florets and salmon, close lid and STEAM for 2 minutes.
4. Quick release. Serve.

Feisty Poached Salmon

Prep time: 20 minutes

Cooking time: 4 minutes

Servings: 4

Nutrients per serving:

Carbohydrates – 4 g

Fat – 24 g

Protein – 0.7 g

Calories – 631

Ingredients:

- 16 ounce salmon fillet, skin on
- 4 scallions, chopped
- Zest of 1 lemon
- ½ tsp of fennel seeds
- 1 tsp white wine vinegar
- 1 bay leaf
- ½ cup dry white wine
- 2 cups chicken broth
- ¼ cup fresh dill
- Salt and pepper, to taste

Instructions:

1. Combine all ingredients in Instant Pot. Stir well.
2. Lock the lid. Cook on HIGH pressure for 4 minutes.
3. Release pressure naturally over 10 minutes. Serve.

Garlic and Almond Butter Swordfish

Prep time: 20 minutes

Cooking time: 25 minutes

Servings: 4

Nutrients per serving:

Carbohydrates – 1 g

Fat – 26 g

Protein – 34 g

Calories – 379

Ingredients:

- 5 sword fish fillets
- ½ cup melted almond butter
- 6 garlic cloves, chopped
- 1 Tbsp black pepper

Instructions:

1. In a bowl, combine garlic, pepper, and melted butter. Mix well.
2. Place fish fillets on parchment paper, one piece per sheet.
3. Cover with butter mix and wrap fish.
4. Repeat the same process with all fish fillets.
5. Transfer to Instant Pot and lock lid.
6. Cook on HIGH pressure for 25 minutes.
7. Release pressure naturally over 10 minutes. Serve.

Spicy Chili Salmon

Prep time: 20 minutes

Cooking time: 2 minutes

Servings: 6

Nutrients per serving:

Carbohydrates – 22 g

Fat – 23 g

Protein – 30 g

Calories – 461

Ingredients:

- 1 lb salmon fillet, cut into 4 pieces
- Salt and pepper to taste
- 1 Tbsp chili powder
- 1 tsp ground cumin
- 1 tsp garlic powder
- 1 avocado, diced
- 1 tsp lime juice
- 1 tsp chopped cilantro
- 1 cup water

Instructions:

1. Pour in 1 cup of water to the pot. Place a steamer rack on top.
2. In a small bowl, combine ground cumin, chili powder, garlic powder.
3. Transfer the fillets to a rack and rub with the mixture.
4. Lock the lid and cook on HIGH pressure for 2 minutes.
5. Naturally release the pressure.
6. Top with avocado, lime juice, and cilantro and serve.

Kale Salad and Salmon

Prep time: 25 minutes

Cooking time: 15 minutes

Servings: 6

Nutrients per serving:

Carbohydrates – 12 g

Fat – 14 g

Protein – 16 g

Calories – 234

Ingredients:

- 1 lemon, juiced
- 2 medium salmon fillets
- ¼ cup extra virgin olive oil
- 1 tsp Dijon mustard
- 4 cups kale, thinly sliced, ribs removed
- 1 tsp salt
- 1 avocado, diced
- 1 cup pomegranate seeds
- 1 cup walnuts, toasted
- 1 cup goat Parmesan cheese, shredded

Instructions:

1. Season salmon with salt.
2. Place a trivet in the Instant Pot.
3. Place salmon on a trivet.
4. Lock the lid. Cook on HIGH pressure for 15 minutes.

5. Release pressure naturally over 10 minutes.
6. Transfer salmon to serving platter.
7. In a bowl, combine kale and salt.
8. In a separate bowl, combine lemon juice, Dijon mustard, olive oil to make the dressing.
9. Mix kale with dressing and add diced avocado, walnuts, cheese, and pomegranate seeds.
10. Toss and serve with the fish.

Halibut Fillets with Lemon

Prep time: 25 minutes

Cooking time: 8 minutes

Servings: 4

Nutrients per serving:

Carbohydrates – 4 g

Fat – 56 g

Protein – 58 g

Calories – 770

Ingredients:

- 4 halibut fillets
- 2 lemon, sliced
- 2 Tbsp chili pepper flakes
- Salt, pepper, to taste
- 1 cup water

Instructions:

1. Put a steamer basket in the Instant Pot.
2. Add a cup of water to Instant Pot.
3. Season fillets with chili pepper, salt, and pepper.
4. Place the seasoned salmon on the trivet and lock lid.
5. Cook on HIGH pressure for 8 minutes.
6. Release pressure naturally over 10 minutes. Serve.

POULTRY

Italian Chicken Dish

Prep time: 25 minutes

Cooking time: 15 minutes

Servings: 4

Nutrients per serving:

Carbohydrates – 19 g

Fat – 6 g

Protein – 7 g

Calories –261

Ingredients:

- 1 Tbsp olive oil
- Black pepper, to taste
- 2 pounds boneless, skinless chicken breasts, cubed
- 4 garlic cloves, minced
- 2½ cups low-sodium chicken stock
- 2 cups coconut cream
- 1 tsp nutmeg, ground
- ½ cup low-fat parmesan, grated
- 1 Tbsp basil, chopped

Instructions:

1. Set Instant Pot to Saute and add oil, allow to heat up.
2. Add chicken and brown for 2-3 minutes.
3. Add garlic, cream, and nutmeg and stir.
4. Lock the lid. Cook on HIGH pressure for 12 minutes.
5. Release pressure naturally over 10 minutes
6. Open the lid and add cheese.
7. Toss well and serve garnished with basil.

Salsa Chicken Breast

Prep time: 25 minutes

Cooking time: 15 minutes

Servings: 4

Nutrients per serving:

Carbohydrates – 19 g

Fat – 6 g

Protein – 7 g

Calories –261

Ingredients:

- 4 chicken breasts
- 2 cups salsa
- 1 lime, juiced
- Salt, pepper, to taste

Instructions:

1. Season chicken with salt and pepper.
2. Add salsa to the Instant Pot.
3. Add chicken on top with lime juice.
4. Lock the lid. Cook on HIGH pressure for 15 minutes.
5. Release the pressure naturally over 10 minutes. Serve.

Caramelized Onion Chicken

Prep time: 25 minutes

Cooking time: 25 minutes

Servings: 4

Nutrients per serving:

Carbohydrates – 42 g

Fat – 19 g

Protein – 42 g

Calories –418

Ingredients:

- 4 chicken breasts
- 4 onions, sliced
- 2 Tbsp almond butter
- 1 Tbsp olive oil
- ½ tsp dried thyme
- ½ cup dry white wine vinegar
- 1 cup chicken stock

Instructions:

1. Set Instant Pot to Saute mode and add butter, let it melt.
2. Add thyme, oil, onion, and Saute for 10 minutes.
3. Stir in vinegar, stock, salt, and pepper and stir.
4. Place the chicken on top.
5. Lock the lid. Cook on HIGH pressure for 15 minutes.
6. Release pressure naturally over 10 minutes. Serve.

Balsamic and Cranberry Chicken

Prep time: 25 minutes

Cooking time: 20 minutes

Servings: 4

Nutrients per serving:

Carbohydrates – 12 g

Fat – 16 g

Protein – 37 g

Calories –343

Ingredients:

- 2 lbs boneless, skinless chicken thighs
- 1 Tbsp olive oil
- ½ a tsp salt
- Pepper, to taste
- ½ small red onion, diced
- 1 cup sugar-free cranberry juice
- 3 Tbsp balsamic vinegar
- 1 Tbsp coconut aminos
- ½ a Tbsp garlic powder
- ½ a Tbsp dried rosemary

Instructions:

1. Set pot to Saute mode and add oil, let it heat up.
2. Season chicken thighs with pepper and salt. Brown on each side for 4-5 minutes.
3. Add in red onion and cook for 4-5 minutes.
4. In a bowl, combine remaining ingredients.
5. Add the mix to the Instant Pot.
6. Lock the lid. Cook on HIGH pressure for 10 minutes.
7. Quick release pressure.
8. Season with salt and pepper. Serve with a sauce that it makes while cooking.

Orange Chicken

Prep time: 20 minutes

Cooking time: 25 minutes

Servings: 4

Nutrients per serving:

Carbohydrates – 8 g

Fat – 15 g

Protein – 41 g

Calories –338

Ingredients:

- 6 chicken thighs
- 2 garlic cloves, minced
- 1 shallot, sliced
- 2 Tbsp olive oil
- 2 orange, cut into segments
- 1 tsp orange zest
- 1 cup chicken stock
- Salt, pepper, to taste

Instructions:

1. Set pot to Saute mode and add chicken, cook until all sides are browned.
2. Stir in remaining ingredients.
3. Lock the lid. Cook on HIGH pressure for 12 minutes.
4. Release the pressure naturally over 10 minutes. Serve.

Lemon Pepper Chicken and Cauliflower Scrambl

Prep time: 25 minutes

Cooking time: 25 minutes

Servings: 4

Nutrients per serving:

Carbohydrates – 1 g

Fat – 20 g

Protein – 20 g

Calories – 270

Ingredients:

- 3 lemons, zested and juiced
- 1 tsp of garlic powder
- 1½ tsp of black pepper
- 2 Tbsp ghee
- 1 tsp salt
- 2 lbs chicken thighs, bone in
- 1 cup chicken broth
- 4 cups large cauliflower florets

Instructions:

1. Set pot to Saute mode.
2. Add in chicken and cook for about 10 minutes until all sides are browned.
3. Stir in remaining ingredients.
4. Lock the lid. Cook on HIGH pressure for 12 minutes.
5. Release the pressure naturally over 10 minutes. Serve.

BEEF, LAMB & PORK

Garlic Pulled Pork

Prep time: 25 minutes

Cooking time: 5 minutes

Servings: 4

Nutrients per serving:

Carbohydrates – 12 g

Fat – 15 g

Protein – 45 g

Calories – 366

Ingredients:

- 18 oz pork tenderloin
- 1 tsp salt
- ½ tsp pepper
- 1 cup chicken broth
- 8 garlic cloves
- 2 sprigs thyme
- 1 Tbsp fresh oregano

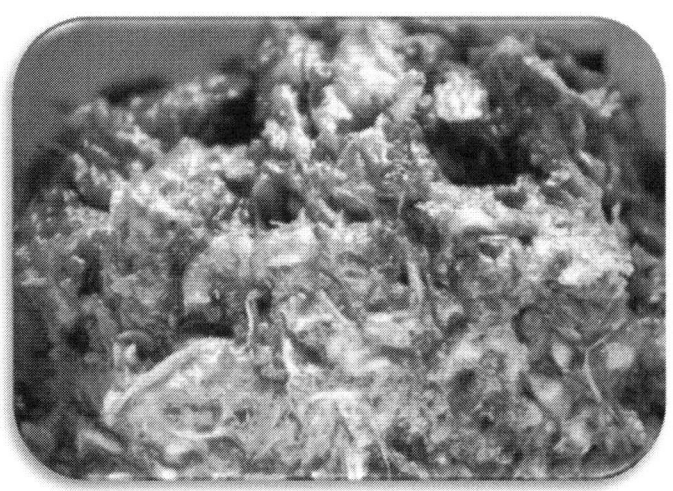

Instructions:

1. Season pork with salt and pepper.
2. Set pot to Saute mode and add olive oil, let it heat up.
3. Add pork loin to Instant Pot and sear all sides.
4. Add remaining ingredients.
5. Lock lid and cook on MEAT/STEW mode for 45 minutes.
6. Release pressure naturally over 10 minutes.
7. Open lid and shred pork. Serve.

Harissa Beef

Prep time: 25 minutes

Cooking time: 25 minutes

Servings: 4

Nutrients per serving:

Carbohydrates – 0.7 g

Fat – 14 g

Protein – 69 g

Calories – 427

Ingredients:

- 4 lb beef roast, trimmed
- 4 garlic cloves, minced
- 1 tsp ground cumin
- 1 tsp ground coriander
- ½ tsp chili powder
- 2 Tbsp Harissa paste
- 1 cup beef stock

Instructions:

1. In a bowl, combine garlic, salt, cumin, salt, coriander, chili powder, and harissa paste.
2. Spread mix over beef and rub in.
3. Transfer meat to Instant Pot and add the stock.
4. Lock the lid. Cook on HIGH pressure for 25 minutes.
5. Release pressure naturally over 10 minutes. Serve.

Original Swedish Pork Roast

Prep time: 25 minutes

Cooking time: 1 hour 30 minutes

Servings: 4

Nutrients per serving:

Carbohydrates – 6 g

Fat – 7 g

Protein – 48 g

Calories – 287

Ingredients:

- 4 lbs boneless pork loin roast
- 1 Tbsp olive oil
- 2 cups low-sodium beef broth
- 1 large yellow onion, grated
- 8 garlic cloves, crushed
- 3 Tbsp swerve
- 2 Tbsp salt
- 1 Tbsp fresh parsley, chopped
- 1 tsp organic ground cumin powder
- ½ tsp organic ground cardamom powder
- 1 tsp fresh ground nutmeg
- 1 tsp black pepper

Instructions:

1. Season pork loin roast with swerve, salt, cardamom powder, cumin powder, and pepper.
2. Set pot to Saute mode and add olive oil.
3. Stir in garlic and onion and cook for 4 minutes.
4. Add pork roast and sear all sides.
5. Stir in beef broth and lock lid.
6. Cook on HIGH pressure for 85 minutes.
7. Naturally release the pressure over 10 minutes.
8. Transfer roast to serving platter and let it rest for 10 minutes.
9. Slice and pour cooking liquid over the slices. Serve.

Balsamic Pork

Prep time: 25 minutes

Cooking time: 20 minutes

Servings: 4

Nutrients per serving:

Carbohydrates – 6 g

Fat – 5 g

Protein – 18 g

Calories – 152

Ingredients:

- 2 lbs pork tenderloin
- ½ cup chicken stock
- 3 Tbsp balsamic vinegar
- 1 thyme sprig
- 1 bay leaf
- Salt, pepper, to taste

Instructions:

1. Season pork with salt and pepper.
2. Transfer loin to Instant Pot.
3. Add rest of the ingredients and stir.
4. Lock the lid. Cook on HIGH pressure for 20 minutes.
5. Release pressure naturally over 10 minutes. Serve.

Majestic Pepper Steak

Prep time: 20 minutes

Cooking time: 20 minutes

Servings: 4

Nutrients per serving:

Carbohydrates – 5 g

Fat – 15 g

Protein – 36 g

Calories – 222

Ingredients:

- 1 lb boneless beef eye round steak
- 80 oz mushrooms, sliced
- 1 red pepper, sliced
- 1 Tbsp garlic, minced
- 1 pack onion soup mix
- 1 Tbsp sesame oil
- 1 cup water

Instructions:

1. Add all ingredients to Instant Pot and gently stir.
2. Lock the lid. Cook on HIGH pressure for 20 minutes.
3. Release pressure naturally over 10 minutes. Serve warm.

Capsicum Braised Pork

Prep time: 20 minutes

Cooking time: 20 minutes

Servings: 4

Nutrients per serving:

Carbohydrates – 2.8 g

Fat – 24 g

Protein – 26 g

Calories – 364

Ingredients:

- 2 lbs pork shoulder
- 1½ tsp dried sage
- 1 cup dry white wine
- ½ cup apple cider
- 1 bay leaf
- Salt, pepper, to taste
- 1 tsp cumin seeds

Instructions:

1. Season slightly the pork with salt, pepper, and cumin.
2. Transfer seasoned meat to Instant Pot.
3. Add vinegar and cider.
4. Lock the lid. Cook on HIGH pressure for 20 minutes.
5. Release pressure naturally over 10 minutes.
6. Let it cool, then slice and serve.

Red Wine Braised Beef Shorts

Prep time: 20 minutes

Cooking time: 1 hour

Servings: 4

Nutrients per serving:

Carbohydrates – 7 g

Fat – 30 g

Protein – 12 g

Calories – 359

Ingredients:

- 4 lb beef short ribs
- ½ Tbsp salt
- 1 Tbsp olive oil
- 1 medium onion, quartered
- 6 cloves garlic ,minced
- 1 cup red wine
- 1 Tbsp red wine vinegar
- 1 cup beef broth
- 1 Tbsp fresh rosemary

Instructions:

1. Season ribs with salt and pepper.
2. Set pot to Saute mode and add olive oil, let it heat up.
3. Add ribs and brown all sides.
4. Work in batches if you are not able to fit all the ribs at once.
5. Add remaining ingredients, coating ribs well.
6. Lock lid and cook on MEAT/STEW mode for 45 minutes.
7. Release pressure naturally over 10 minutes.
8. Serve with cooking sauce.

Artichoke and Lemon Pork Chops

Prep time: 20 minutes

Cooking time: 30 minutes

Servings: 4

Nutrients per serving:

Carbohydrates – 5 g

Fat – 26 g

Protein – 10 g

Calories – 286

Ingredients:

- 3 oz bacon, diced
- 4½ inch thick bone-in pork chops
- 2 tsp ground black pepper
- 1 shallot, minced
- 1 tsp lemon zest
- 3 garlic cloves, minced
- 1 tsp dried rosemary
- 1 cup chicken broth
- 1 9-oz package frozen artichoke heart quarters

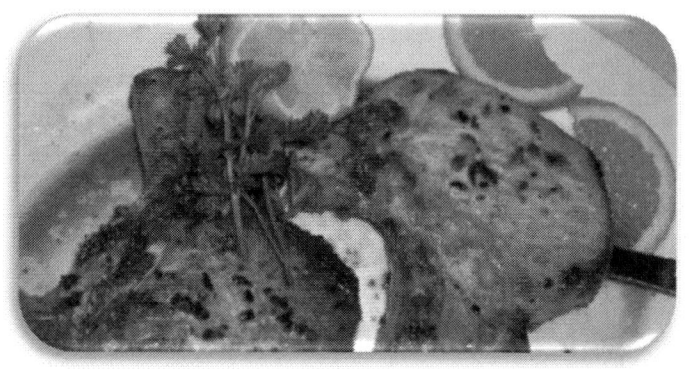

Instructions:

1. Set pot to Saute mode and add bacon.
2. Cook for 5 minutes, until the fat is rendered and the bacon is crispy.
3. Transfer bacon to plate.
4. Season the chops with pepper and salt and transfer to Pot.
5. Brown the chops in batches if needed.
6. Add shallots and cook for 1 minute.
7. Add lemon zest, rosemary, and garlic and cook until fragrant.
8. Add chicken broth, artichokes, cooked bacon, and stir.
9. Nestle the chops back to the sauce.
10. Lock the lid. Cook on HIGH pressure on MEAT/STEW settings for 15 minutes.
11. Perform a quick release.
12. Open the lid and season with salt and pepper.
13. Serve with the lemon artichoke sauce.

Pineapple Pork Chops

Prep time: 25 minutes

Cooking time: 35 minutes

Servings: 4

Nutrients per serving:

Carbohydrates – 101 g

Fat – 15 g

Protein – 24 g

Calories – 621

Ingredients:

- 6 thin cut pork chops
- Balsamic glaze
- Seasonings of your choice
- Olive oil, as needed
- ½ pineapple, cubed
- 1 cup water

Instructions:

1. Season pork chops generously.
2. Set pot to Saute mode and drizzle virgin olive oil to the bottom of the pot.
3. Let it heat up.
4. Add pork chops and Saute.
5. Remove chops and layer them on a steam rack/trivet.
6. Glaze the top (reserving a bit for garnishing).
7. Add pineapple chunks (reserving a bit for garnishing) on top of the chops.
8. Pour in a cup of water to Instant Pot.
9. Place trivet in Instant Pot.
10. Lock the lid. Cook on HIGH pressure for about 25 minutes.
11. Naturally release the pressure over 10 minutes.
12. Remove chops and add a bit more glaze and pineapples.

DESSERTS

Original Peppermint Latte

Prep time: 10 minutes

Cooking time: 5 minutes

Servings: 4

Nutrients per serving:

Carbohydrates – 14 g

Fat – 9 g

Protein – 4 g

Calories – 169

Ingredients:

- 4 cups almond milk
- 2 cups coffee
- 1 tsp vanilla bean extract
- 23 drops peppermint oil

Instructions:

1. Add ingredients to Instant Pot.
2. Lock the lid. Cook on HIGH pressure for 5 minutes.
3. Release pressure naturally over 10 minutes. Serve.

Mashed Sweet Potatoes

Prep time: 10 minutes

Cooking time: 10 minutes

Servings: 2

Nutrients per serving:

Carbohydrates – 24 g

Fat – 1 g

Protein – 4 g

Calories – 115

Ingredients:

- 2 pounds garnet sweet potatoes, peeled, cut into 1-inch chunks
- 2-3 Tbsp clarified butter
- 2 Tbsp stevia
- ¼ tsp nutmeg
- 1 cup water
- Salt, as needed

Instructions:

1. Add water to Instant Pot.
2. Place the steamer basket in the pot.
3. Add sweet potato chunks to the pot.
4. Lock the lid. Cook on HIGH pressure for 8 minutes.
5. Quick release pressure.
6. Open the lid and transfer cooked potatoes to a bowl.
7. Use a masher to mash the potatoes.
8. Add remaining ingredients, except salt, and mash well.
9. Season with salt and serve.

Coconut and Avocado Pudding

Prep time: 15 minutes

Cooking time: 5 minutes

Servings: 2

Nutrients per serving:

Carbohydrates – 74 g

Fat – 20 g

Protein – 6 g

Calories – 432

Ingredients:

- 2 avocados, pitted, peeled and chopped
- 2 tsp vanilla bean extract
- 2 Tbsp coconut sugar
- 1 Tbsp lime juice
- 1 14.5-oz can coconut milk
- 1½ cups water

Instructions:

1. In a bowl, combine all ingredients.
2. Pour mix into ramekins.
3. Add water to Instant Pot.
4. Place a steamer basket in Instant Pot.
5. Add ramekins to the basket.
6. Lock the lid. Cook on HIGH pressure for 5 minutes.
7. Release pressure naturally over 10 minutes. Serve.

Matcha Coconut Cream

Prep time: 15 minutes

Cooking time: 4 minutes

Servings: 2

Nutrients per serving:

Carbohydrates – 7 g

Fat – 2 g

Protein – 4 g

Calories – 181

Ingredients:

- 4 Tbsp coconut milk
- 1 cup fat-free coconut cream
- 3 Tbsp hot water
- 4 ½ tsp green tea powder

Instructions:

1. Combine all ingredients in Instant Pot.
2. Whisk gently and lock lid.
3. Cook on HIGH pressure for 4 minutes.
4. Quick release pressure.
5. Divide mix amongst small ramekins and chill for 15 minutes. Serve.

CONCLUSION

Thank you for reading this book and having the patience to try the recipes.

I do hope that you gain as much enjoyment reading and experimenting with the meals as I have had writing this book.

If you would like to leave a comment, you can do it at the Order section->Digital orders, in your amazon account.

Stay safe and healthy!

Recipe Index

Conversion Tables

VALUE EQUIVALENTS (LIQUID)

US STANDARD	US STANDARD (OUNCES)	METRIC (VOLUME)
2 tablespoons	1 fl. oz.	30 mL
1/4 cup	2 fl. oz.	60 mL
1/2 cup	4 fl. oz.	120 mL
1 cup	8 fl. oz.	240mL
1 1/2 cup	12 fl. oz.	355 mL
2 cups or 1 pint	16 fl. oz.	`475 mL
4 cups or 1 quart	32 fl. oz.	1 L
1 gallon	128 fl. oz.	4 L

VALUE EQUIVALENTS (LIQUID)

US STANDARD	METRIC (APPROXIMATE)
$1/8$ teaspoon	0.5 mL
1/4 teaspoon	1 mL
1/2 teaspoon	2 mL
$2/3$ teaspoon	4 mL
1 teaspoon	5 mL
1 tablespoon	15 mL
1/4 cup	59 mL
$1/3$ cup	79 mL
1/2 cup	118 mL
$2/3$ cup	156 mL
3/4 cup	177 mL
1 cup	235 mL
2 cups or 1 pint	475 mL
3 cups	700 mL
4 cups or 1 quart	1 L
1/2 gallon	2 L
1 gallon	4 L

OVEN TEMPERATURES

FAHRENHEIT(F)	CELSIUS(C) APPROXIMATE
250 °F	120 °C
300 °F	150 °C
325 °F	165 °C
350 °F	180 °C
375 °F	190°C
400 °F	200 °C
425 °F	220 °C
450 °F	230 °C

WEIGHT EQUIVALENTS

US STANDARD	METRIC (APPROXIMATE)
1/2 ounce	15 g
1 ounces	30 g
2 ounces	60 g
4 ounces	115 g
8 ounces	225 g
12 ounces	340 g
16 ounce or 1 pound	455 g

Made in the USA
San Bernardino, CA
17 July 2019